D0593652

JOAN
CHITTISTER

The
Sacred
IN-BETWEEN

Spiritual wisdom for life's every moment

FOR MORE INFORMATION
ABOUT JOAN CHITTISTER, OSB,
PLEASE VISIT HER WEBSITE:
www.joanchittister.org

Third Printing 2014
TWENTY-THIRD PUBLICATIONS
A Division of Bayard
One Montauk Avenue, Suite 200
New London, CT 06320
(860) 437-3012 or (800) 321-0411
www.23rdpublications.com

Copyright ©2013 Joan Chittister. All rights reserved. No part of
this publication may be reproduced in any manner without prior
written permission of the publisher. Write to the Permissions
Editor.

ISBN 978-1-62785-001-8
Library of Congress Control Number: 2013944790

Printed in the U.S.A.

Contents

Chapter One

Life is what happens to you

IN THE BOOK OF LIFE,
THE ANSWERS AREN'T IN THE BACK.
Charlie Brown –Peanuts

"When you get what you like in life," one of our old nuns was fond of repeating to the novices, "Jesus smiles at you. When you don't get what you like," she went on, "Jesus reaches down and kisses you."

It's not a theology I'd teach with much gusto today, but I got her point. There are things that look very bad for us — in fact, that are very bad for us — that confuse us and anger us and depress us, but which, in the end, do more for us than sunny days and endless fortune and limitless luck can ever do.

John Lennon put it another way: "Life is what happens to you while you're busy making other plans." And who doesn't know the truth of that one?

You plan to go back to college and the recession comes and there's no money for that kind of thing anymore. Now what do you do?

Your mother-in-law is babysitting so you can go on working and she gets cancer. Now what happens to the baby?

You're already beginning to look for the retirement condo in Florida and your spouse dies. There's no one to retire with anymore. Now what happens to the rest of life?

Indeed, there are no answers at the end of the book of life. No quick fixes. No ways around the tough parts. Instead, life is what we learn as we live it. And what we learn, as we live it, is what tests and shapes the mettle of our souls.

There is no way to comprehend how to go through grief other than by going through it. There is no way to practice foregoing the hot rage that comes with feeling ignored or dismissed or found to be "essentially disordered"—for any reason. There

2

is no way to plan for the sense of abandonment you feel in a society that thinks differently from you: because your child is gay, maybe, or because you're a woman and so automatically considered deficient for the work, perhaps, or because you're not white in a white world, or because the person you thought was an eternal friend abandoned you.

Those things we need to figure out for ourselves, one situation at a time.

But then, once we have been through those dark and raw moments in life, we discover a newer, better kind of sweetness. We not only find out who other people are; we find out what we are too. We find out not only how weak we feel but also how strong we can really be in the face of endless pain or mockery or bigotry or the shallowness of self-righteous morality.

Then, we discover that life is not a terminal disease. On the contrary, it is always, and at best, a time of endless development, of choosing to be either more or less than we thought we could be.

Then, we know not only the answers to the hard periods of life; we know that no question can ever defeat us, can ever make us less than the best of ourselves again.

✳ "There's no way out but through," the wag said. What the wag didn't say, however, is that there are some things that, without having gone through them, not even we will be able to know the full truth of ourselves.

✳ It's not important to answer every question in life. Most of them aren't worth struggling with. They come today and disappear tomorrow. "It is not every question that deserves an answer," the Roman philosopher Syrus wrote. Let them go.

✳ Beware those who never doubt that there may be answers beyond their own. They can be very dangerous for the rest of us. "Great evil," Lynn Andrews wrote, "has been done on earth by people who think they have all the answers."

✳ It takes a great deal of strength to refuse to answer anything of importance too quickly. It is often better to let a newly emerging question answer itself over time than to insist on dealing with it from perspectives too old to be useful to the present situation.

✳ We grow in life to greater emotional and moral stature, not because of what we think we know, but because of what we know we don't. "Life," Florida Scott-Maxwell writes, "does not accommodate you, it shatters you. It is meant to. And it couldn't do it better. Every seed destroys its container or else there would be no fruition."

✳ Life is about doing the best you can in the moment in which you find yourself, so that, eventually, you can find yourself even wiser than you now are.

✳ To look at life's problems—nuclear proliferation, the pollution of the seas, the oppression of women, the starvation of peoples—as if they belonged to someone else other than ourselves is the greatest of all moral immaturities.

❊ There is no similarity whatsoever between being accepting of difficulty and being resigned to it. Where injustice or pain or oppression exists in my life, I must struggle, so as to free those who come after me from what I myself could not avoid.

❊ Life is not meant to be perfect. It is meant to be perfectly capable of challenging us to be everything we are meant to be.

❊ Life is one long list of instructions, none of which are ever eternally true. Which means that sometimes you simply have to trust yourself.

❊ The problem with life is not that we find ourselves in one challenging situation after another. The problem comes when we face no challenges at all. Then we never exercise our mind and soul enough to equal the growth of our bodies.

✤ Don't expect to be given a blueprint to lead you through life. We all create our own.

✤ It is not what we've been taught that makes the difference as we go through life. It is the choices we make for ourselves when we are finally forced to choose among them.

✤ Life does not get easier as we go along. It only gets to be a question so great that we have no choice but to trust that its answer will be as profound as the problems it poses. Albert Schweitzer said of it: "As we acquire more knowledge, things do not become more comprehensible, but more mysterious."

✤ It's not a matter of going through life; it is a matter of growing steadily deeper, always broader, forever wiser.

✤ Do not aspire to know it all. Aspire to listen to it all and to respond with compassion. It is only compassion that makes life livable for anybody.

❋ Life is at best an invitation to begin and begin and begin—all over again. It's when we cease to begin that we cease to be fully alive.

❋ Discovering our purpose in life is never complete unless we discover it in relation to the rest of the world around us. Anything other than that leaves us with a very small purpose in a very small world called "me."

❋ Discovering ourselves is often a very slow, very accidental process. People study all their early lives to become one thing and then, along the way, become something very other. Then, we know that the self has trumped the straight-jacket of other people's "expectations."

❋ To be an eternal learner is to live every moment of life fully alive. We never know it all. We can never know too much. We can never be happy by becoming static. When we stop growing, we stop being really alive.

✻ Folk literature explains the need for challenge both succinctly and poignantly for those who are denied the opportunity to be anything they feel they are called to be in society. "Old lady," the young woman asks, "what is a woman's greatest burden?" And the old woman answers her: "Young woman, the greatest burden in life is to have no burden to carry at all."

✻ Very little of what we learn now will still be considered current knowledge ten years from now. Which means that none of us can rest on last year's information. "In times of change," Eric Hoffer wrote, "learners inherit the earth, while the learned find themselves beautifully equipped to deal with a world that no longer exists."

✻ Don't be afraid of the unknown. It is, in fact, the doorway to the future. "The illiterate of the 21st century," Alvin Toffler said, "will not be those who cannot read and write, but those who cannot learn, unlearn, and relearn."

❊ Life in our times demands new respect for creativity. We must now begin to earn our bread differently, live differently, learn differently, and imagine the future differently. It's time to strike out and make life what we want it to be.

❊ Don't wait for someone else to tell you what you should become. Become *it* a piece at a time. Follow your interests and inclinations, and watch your life become what you always wanted it to be.

❊ Never despair of life. It does not depend on what you get in life; it depends on what you do that makes you happy. The artist Pablo Picasso tells us, "I am always doing that which I cannot do in order that I may learn how to do it."

Chapter Two

Plans

I'M ONLY LOST IF I'M GOING
SOMEPLACE IN PARTICULAR.
Megan M. Scribner

L ife, we learn young—or at least I did—is
about planning. They taught us to keep
lists so we wouldn't forget anything. We
learned to keep a calendar so we'd get to the right
place at the right time. We were required to take
courses in one school in such a way that we could
get into another one, this time in business or en-
gineering or liberal arts or science or whatever. We
were told to know where we were going in life and
then plan how we intended to get there.

But the lesson that lingered beyond all the others was the one that came in a kind of child's dog-

gerel. I said it over and over again for years:

For want of a nail, the shoe was lost;
For want of a shoe, the horse was lost;
For want of a horse, the rider was lost;
For want of a rider, the battle was lost;
For want of a battle, the kingdom was lost;
And all for the want of a horseshoe nail.
AUTHOR UNKNOWN

No doubt about it, this planning stuff was important. This careful organization of all the parts of life was crucial. This learning to be in control, to make sure no mistakes were ever made, was surely the key to success, to happiness, to fulfillment. No mention, of course, of all the things we can't ever control. Like death or loss or failure or trauma or calamity—or just plain circumstances in life.

Learning to redirect, to go with the flow, to accept the unacceptable when the direction goes awry, is every bit as important—maybe in the end a great deal more important—as learning to insist on having life just as we planned it.

I know only one thing: If my father hadn't died and my mother hadn't remarried, and if we hadn't moved where we would never have thought of go-ing, and if I hadn't injured my arm the very day I had planned to go out for the basketball team and then joined the journalism staff instead, I wouldn't be writing these words to you right now. Or, as the Chinese say, "Good event; bad event? Who knows?"

Learning to let go, learning to find our way by other directions, staying open to new ways and new paths and new ideas, is, more often than not, the only way there is to get where we are really meant to go.

....

❋ When we need to know every result
   of every new thing before we'll even
   think of trying, it is a sign that God is
   still a question mark in our lives.

❋ The God who goes with us in light
   is the same God who companions us
   through the dark spots. That's the God
   the light is meant to teach us to trust.

❋ When a person needs to control every iota

13

of every idea, they squeeze every ounce of creativity out of every possibility. These are not the people who can lead us to tomorrow.

❈ Planning is a very good thing—as long as it doesn't choke the life out of each exciting possibility.

❈ It's always good to leave a few questions unanswered at the beginning of every project. That way, there is always the opportunity to make better plans as we go.

❈ Life does not come preplanned. It comes in the form of unshaped clay. The shaping of it by trial and error is left to us. That's why clay is soft.

❈ Giving up one plan for another is not failure. It is the recognition that God is still at work in us.

❈ To insist on knowing the end of something at the beginning of it is to play God without either the script or the talent for it.

❊ Some people confuse leadership with authority. Leadership opens doors so we can find the best of ourselves in the journey itself. Authority draws maps so we can live their old ideas instead of our own new ones.

❊ There is no such thing as failure. There is only the need to begin again— more experienced than before.

❊ There's a big difference between a plan and an instruction. A plan says where I'm going; an instruction tells me how I'm supposed to get there—whether I discover, en route, that there is a better way or not.

❊ Thinking a thing through and planning how to do each part of it are not the same. One enables us to imagine what we will need to complete the journey, whatever changes we may need to make on the way. The other sets us on a road no one has

ever been on before with an old map for
a guide and not a clue about where else
this road might take us on the way.

❈ Certainty is no substitute for creativity.
Creative people make the road as they go.
Others stay where they're told and go no-
where different in the end. As the Chinese
say, "If we do not change our direction, we
are likely to end up where we are headed."

❈ Every life is a unique challenge to which
no other life is the answer. "There was
the Door/to which I found no key,"
Omar Khayyam writes; "There was the
Veil/through which I might not see."
We must come to realize that the un-
knowns in life are the dimensions of it
that will really determine both its challenges and the quality we bring to it.

❈ When what we expect does not happen, life in its fullness is about to begin.
It's what we do then that counts, not

what we said we'd do but couldn't.

❋ Going into the unknown teaches us more
about life and more about ourselves than
anything stable and defined can ever do.
"Uncertainty and expectation," William
Congreve writes, "are the joys of life."

❋ Those who cannot leave the beaten path
cannot lead the world to a new one. "One
doesn't discover new lands," André Gide
said, "without consenting to lose sight
of the shore for a very long time."

❋ It isn't newness that leads the world to
despair; it is rigidity that leads to at-
rophy. "I postpone death," Anaïs Nin
writes, "by living, by suffering, by error, by risking, by giving, by losing."

❋ We don't fall into ruts in life; we dig them for
ourselves. We settle in; we withdraw from
other people; we stop trying new foods,
new friends, new places, new books, new

ideas, new events. We just curl up within ourselves. We stop trying. Or more to the point: we stop living long before we die. And in the doing of it, without realizing it, perhaps, we stop the search for God.

❈ If you are not where you thought you would be at this stage of life, you are, nevertheless, where God is waiting to find you.

❈ Maybe only gardeners really know what it means to plant something and wait to see if anything will come from it. But all of life is like that. If you are not planting something new in your life right now, you have ceased to be the part of ongoing creation God meant for all of us to be.

❈ When we don't know something and can't figure it out, that is the very point at which new life awaits us. "The most beautiful experience we can have," Albert Einstein wrote, "is the mysterious. It...stands at the cradle of true art and true science."

✳ The simplest, apparently dullest of lives
is a mystery. We are all meant to pen-
etrate the marrow of life until we can realize how clearly purposeful is our own.
And then we must race, however few
our days, to complete that purpose.

✳ We are all meant to be creators of life—our
own—to the very edge of its boundar-
ies. But that means being willing to risk
a tomorrow that is different than today.

✳ If God had thought that "plans" were
the center, the core, the heart, the sum-
mit, of life, God would never have
made evolution the process of it.

✳ Being willing to keep on growing, keep
on going into the dark alleys of life, is
to live life to the full all the way to the
end. As Charles Lamb put it: "Nothing
puzzles me more than time and space;
yet nothing troubles me less."

Chapter Three

Love
remains

Amo Ergo Sum: I LOVE, THEREFORE I AM!
Kathleen Raine

I want to tell you about Gloria and Edgar. Gloria was the unsightliest girl in the class. Edgar lived down the street and was what we then called "the deaf and dumb mute."

But first I want to tell you about philosophy.

Philosophers are people who ponder the great questions of life, spin one or more of all the possible answers to them, and then leave the rest of us to wander up and down the highways and by-ways of our worlds trying to figure out which one of those answers, for us, was the best of them all.

What is truth? Socrates asked. What is the answer to pain? the stoics asked. What is the best possible human organization? Rousseau asked. What is a woman? Simone de Beauvoir asked. How do we know we really exist? Descartes asked.

As a young college student, I remember being deeply impressed by the entire exercise. What kind of person did it take to be a philosopher? How was it possible for someone as pedestrian as I to understand such things?

Then, I got older and discovered that, as a matter of fact, we all ask those questions. In fact, we spend a good portion of life trying to figure life out. We don't always know we're doing it, of course, but we do it just the same. More than that, we often do it when we're very young and it shapes the rest of our lives.

Which brings me back to Gloria and Edgar.

Gloria was a very plain girl in a world of social stars. The "popular girls" in the class decided who was "in" and who was "out" of social acceptance. The rest of the girls simply came to school—but they never got to the parties. They didn't sit at the lunch table where the in-crowd sat. And Gloria was definitely not "in." She took the butt of the jokes, the snide remarks, the snubs that came as invitations flew around her and she never got one. But Gloria didn't wilt under the exclusions. Instead, she threw her own parties, planned her own social events—and invited everyone.

Edgar spent his life being made fun of by the other kids for his stumbling walk and the strange sounds he made. But Edgar smiled at them anyway. He just laughed and spent his days helping old people on the block carry their groceries or empty their garbage cans every day of his life.

I don't remember most of the other girls in the class. I never did know the rest of the people on the block. But I've never been able to forget Gloria and Edgar.

That's how I know that the great philosopher René Descartes was wrong when he said as proof that he was alive, "I think, therefore I am." No, thinking does not make us fully alive. Instead, on this question, Kathleen Raine, a philosopher like the rest of us, is the one who has really found the answer. She writes, "*Amo ergo sum:* I love, therefore I am!"

Love is the great definer of life. Those who love, live. Those who live and never learn to love are already dead of soul. Love something; love anything and everything in order to release the best of yourself. No doubt about it: It is love that makes us human. I doubt that Kathleen Raine knows Gloria and Edgar but if she's ever asked to explain how she arrived at such a profound philosophical conclusion, these two life-loving people are surely it.

....

⁕ Learning to love is the challenge of a lifetime because it requires us to think about something other than ourselves.

⁕ Learning to be lovable is an even greater challenge because it requires that we make ourselves a joy to others.

⁕ Learning to do both makes us experts at life. "The greatest thing you'll ever learn," Eden Ahbez writes, "is just to love and be loved in return."

❋ Neither love nor lovableness comes without concentration and commitment. The problem is that there are very seductive but superficial imitations of both of them. But in the end, the differences between them are clear: "It is love," Augustine of Hippo tells us, "that asks, that seeks, that knocks, that finds, and that is faithful to what it finds."

❋ Love requires us to make something other than ourselves the center of our lives. Clearly it is a learned art.

❋ Without love, we isolate ourselves from life. However much we race from party to party, something is clearly missing. "The opposite of loneliness," Richard Bach writes, "is not togetherness; it's intimacy."

❋ It's easy to find a crowd to run around with. It's one of the miracles of life, though, to find someone with whom we can share our souls. "Where there is the greatest love," Willa Cather wrote, "there are always miracles."

⁂ To love someone is to double all our joys and divide all our disappointments. To be loved is to increase our courage and decrease our fears.

⁂ To love another for our own sake, rather than theirs, is to go through life a perpetual adolescent.

⁂ Real love grows. It is never at its inception what it is later, as it becomes more spiritual, less physical, more one and less two, more supportive than supported.

⁂ Love never counts—either what it gets or what it gives. "Love," Eleanor Farjeon writes, "has no uttermost, as the stars have no number and the sea no rest."

⁂ Love we can't see isn't love. Love shops and cooks and laughs and talks and tells and plans things that the other person really wants. It is the gift I give to someone who either never expects it or has every right to expect it but never requires it.

❊ Being able to reach out with warmth and care to those we do not know is every bit as important as connecting with those we do know. Otherwise, the love we claim to have is only self-centered rather than really human.

❊ Love is the value that trumps all others — truth, equality, even justice. "At the evening of life," John of the Cross writes, "we shall be judged on our love." And the reason is obvious. For the one who loves, dishonesty, oppression, and injustice are impossible.

❊ Once we love the people we serve, the work we do, the life we have, the ones with whom we go through life, we have it all. There is no more. "The most important thing in life," Morrie Schwartz writes, "is to learn how to give out love — and to let it come in."

❊ Love is the cocoon that saves us from the hostility of those whose

negativity turns every moment into
a competition or a put-down.

❋ To go into a group that does not want you,
just take with you one person who loves you,
and nothing can possibly hurt you there.

❋ Love is not about finding someone who is
perfect; it is about finding someone who
understands you perfectly and loves you
regardless. "Contrary to Pascal's saying,"
Jacques Maritain wrote, "we don't love qualities, we love persons, sometimes by reason
of their defects as well as of their qualities."

❋ Truth is time-bound; winning is fleeting;
competition fails us; accumulations go to
dust. Only love remains. Novalis says of it:
"Love works magic/It is the final purpose/of
the world story,/The Amen of the universe."

❋ If you love someone, set them free.
Possessiveness drives the possessed one
away. "Anxiety is love's greatest killer,"

27

Anaïs Nin writes. "It makes one feel as you might when a drowning man holds onto you. You want to save him, but you know he will strangle you with his panic."

✳ The real love of two, if we hold it in healthy hands, makes us fearless, makes us even more loving, expands our hearts rather than contracts them, and so enables us to take in the entire universe. Petrarch tells us, "Love is the crowning grace of humanity, the holiest right of the soul...the redeeming principle that chiefly reconciles the heart to life and is prophetic of eternal good."

✳ Love is all we know of God. It is all the proof we need of God. It is the sight of God in our own lives. "The story of love is not important," Helen Hayes says. "What is important is that one is capable of love. It is perhaps the only glimpse we are permitted of eternity."

Chapter Four

Reflections

DO NOT FREE A CAMEL
OF THE BURDEN OF HIS HUMP;
YOU MAY BE FREEING HIM FROM BEING A CAMEL.

G. K. Chesterton

I remember that the courtship had been a stormy one. I was too young to understand everything that was going on, of course, but the agitation among the aunts and uncles sounded loud and clear, even to a ten-year-old. The family was clearly uncomfortable at the very thought that this latest relationship would end in marriage. Apparently my cousin loved him...but. "But" she wanted him to get a better job. "But" she thought he did a little too much carousing. "But" she thought he wasn't ambitious enough. So they fought about those things all the time. "After we're married, I just know he'll change," she said, half certain, half hopeful. "Listen, Margaret," I heard my mother say back to her, "don't marry somebody you wish were different because you think you can change him once the wedding is over."

The insight stuck with me. People are what they are, and in the end they will surely be it unless they themselves decide otherwise.

But frankly the idea bothered me. After all, shouldn't we shape people into what they ought to be, what they could be if they tried harder, and not simply allow them to be what they want to be? "Water takes the line of least resistance," I'd heard someone say once. I got the message. If allowed to follow our own inclinations, wouldn't we always take the easiest way out?

I never needed my mother's advice as part of the marital selection process, obviously, but as the years went by, I began to realize that it stood a person in good stead in lots of other situations too.

For instance, I had a great student writer in one of my classes. But he liked science better than he liked writing. He wasn't nearly as talented at science as he was at writing, I thought. So I tried everything I could to steer him away from a major in criminology to a major in English. Until I remembered my mother's uncompromising counsel to my cousin: *"Don't think you can change the natural bent of a person and expect them to thank you for it later."* They tell me he's an outstanding policeman now.

The problem, of course, is that it's so easy to do "what's good for a person." It is not always easy to do what is even better for them—like allow them to become the best of what they are.

I came to understand too that forever making smooth a child's path is not always good stress training for the rest of life. Then, when there is no one around to forever lift the load for them, the inclination to quit or collapse under the strain of the ordinary is a greater problem than the problem itself.

Finally, I began to see that after Vatican II—when we began to encourage sisters to do the ministries to which they were most called, both by the needs around them and by the natural talents within them—the community itself became more a center of spiritual dynamism that stretched far beyond itself than simply a parochial labor force, however good the work.

No doubt about it—our full development as human beings depends on our becoming the best of exactly what we know ourselves to be.

The function of a camel's hump is to store fat for the long, hard journey across the desert. If you remove a camel's hump, therefore, you have as good as doomed it to death. And when we repress in ourselves our best gifts because we would prefer to be something other than what we are, we will never be what we could have been. When we set out to hide our essential reality—as in, "No, of course there is no Indian or Black or Irish blood in me"—we deny the very thing that may be our natural talent. When we wrench ourselves into what other people want us to be rather than what we want to do, our real self dies. And then what is the new look worth?

* When we set out to change other people to meet our standards, it is only because we do not intend to change ourselves to meet theirs.

32

✻ What we carry within ourselves are both the gifts we have been given and the challenges we must meet within ourselves.

✻ Highly rigid families, groups, and churches dwarf the possibilities within us in order to achieve their own ends.

✻ Control of the other is the way we make ourselves secure. If I can control the behaviors of others, I save myself from having to change myself.

✻ If we wrench ourselves into what we would like to be rather than what we are, we abort a part of ourselves. As a result, there are whole parts of us that will never come to life.

✻ Life is the process of growing into the fullness of ourselves. "Sitting still, doing nothing, spring comes, and the grass grows by itself," the Zen master taught. The only thing that can really happen to us is already within us.

✳ Like the camel, there are humps on all of us. It's learning to accept them that is the struggle. "Only your friends will tell you," the Sicilian proverb teaches, "when your face is dirty." Thank God if you have friends like that.

✳ Our task is not to change who we are. Our task is to recognize how we have gone about being who we are and then learning how to do it even better—now.

✳ Once we really learn to accept ourselves— to quit posturing, to stop hiding who we are, to stop pretending to be something we are not—we are finally ready to accept others for who they are too.

✳ We are born with everything it takes to be our best selves. It is only when we refuse to accept our limitations that we go through life either frustrated or unhappy. "The fish cannot drown in water," Mechthilde of Magdeburg wrote. So how can we possibly doubt ourselves?

❋ To wish our lives away wanting to be
   something other than who or what we
   are instead of living what we are as hap-
   pily as we can is a terrible waste of life.

❋ We come to be the fullness of ourselves by
   allowing the lives of those around us to call
   us out of ourselves. "If you have come to
   help me, you are wasting your time," the
   Australian aboriginal woman said. "But if you
   have come because your liberation is bound
   up with mine, then let us work together."

❋ Beware of becoming what your friends
   want you to be or you may never become who you are. "No person is your
   friend who demands your silence or de-
   nies your right to grow."—Alice Walker

❋ God never makes the same thing twice.
   Every single thing on earth is un-
   like every other. The point is that our
   humps are not our ugliness. They are
   the sign of our special possibilities.

⁎ We grow up hearing one of two things about ourselves. We hear either how good we are — or how bad we are. What a pity. The truth is that neither position is helpful. What we all need to hear is simply how loved we are, regardless of whether some people consider us either good or bad. As Nathaniel Branden wrote, "No one was ever made 'good' by being informed he or she was 'bad.'"

⁎ Finding out who we really are is the greatest exercise of life. It is our challenge — and ours alone. It is coming to the point where we can claim who we are that is difficult.

⁎ When we accept another person, when we assume that they are doing all that they can do at this particular moment in life, we free them to become more. It's when we label one another, including ourselves, that we limit ourselves. "Accept me as I am," the ancients said, "so I may learn what I may become."

✳ What does it take to help another person grow into the best they can be? A reporter asked Reggie Jackson what makes a person a good manager. Jackson answered: "I'll tell you what makes a great manager. A great manager has a knack for making ballplayers think they are better than they think they are. He forces you to have a good opinion of yourself. He lets you know he believes in you. He makes you get more out of yourself. And once you learn how good you really are, you never settle for playing anything less than your very best."

✳ Trying to be what we aren't makes it impossible to become what we are.

✳ Learning to leave other people alone is one of life's greatest gifts — to them and to us as well.

✳ No amount of education can change what's inside of us. It can only un-leash it. Or as Gertrude Stein put it, "A rose is a rose is a rose."

❊ The major temptation of any system—church or state—is to mold their adherents to what they want them to be rather than free them to become what they are, however difficult the becoming. Agnes Repplier says: "Too much rigidity on the part of teachers should be followed by a brisk spirit of insubordination on the part of the taught."

❊ People do not grow up to be subordinate. They grow up to be adults. To thwart that is a sin against creation.

❊ Whatever we were yesterday, we have the right to be something else tomorrow. The only question is what we will choose to be, whether we will concentrate on what we can do or what we can't do. "The world is new to us every morning," said the Baal Shem Tov; "this is God's gift, and every person should believe they are reborn every day."

Chapter Five

Time

TIME DOES NOT CHANGE US.
IT JUST UNFOLDS US.
Max Frisch

Every country on earth has some kind of cliché or stereotype attached that portends to describe the personality characteristics of its people. Germans are hardworking, the conventional wisdom concludes; the French are romantic; the Irish are fun loving; the Swiss are efficient. The labels go all the way around the globe. And there's a bit of truth to all of them and a lot of error as well. But whatever the balance of truth in the markers, the conviction that there are such things as national characteristics clings to a people like oil on rock. The labels say something about the qualities a people value, about the nature of their culture, about their priorities.

My young father, dead at 25, left nothing behind for me except his prayer book and one prayer card. I read it over and over as a child. It's been gone for years but I remember parts of it yet. It read:

I have only just a minute,
Only 60 seconds in it.
Given to me, didn't choose it.
Mustn't waste it, can't refuse it.
But I must suffer if I lose it.

There was more to that doggerel, of course, but I have forgotten the rest—but not the message. On the contrary, the basic message got through to me and haunted me. It was legacy enough for the rest of my life. The American mantra, I learned, is time.

We are, in fact, obsessed with time. We're a pragmatic, productive people, and time is the national God. It shows in our language. No other people on earth speak of time as we do. We spend time and invest time and need time and lose time and save time and waste time and find time and buy time and gain time and want time. And, in the end, time, not life, threatens to absorb us.

Time, the American assumes, is for doing something, for producing things, for achieving goals. And in our commitment to pragmatism and effectiveness, we far too often fail to realize that life is really about becoming a person of merit and worth.

It might be useful to take a moment each day to give more serious consideration to what we are becoming rather than to what we are doing as time goes by.

....

✳ There is really no such thing as time when something outside ourselves is not pushing us, pulling us from one moment to the next. "Time, when it is left to itself and no definite demands are made on it," Edith Wharton writes, "cannot be trusted to move at any recognized pace." The trick of a hectic life, then, is to keep for ourselves space enough for the soul to bloom alone and in the dark.

⁂ Time is the great teacher. It teaches us to forget what has nothing to do with today and to remember that, whatever happened yesterday, there is still a tomorrow enough to make it right.

⁂ Time carries us from level to level of life, giving every stage of it the wisdom of its own past.

⁂ To hurry through life, running frantically from one thing to another, is to leave the soul behind.

⁂ There is no such thing, psychologists know now, as "multitasking." To do two things at once simply means that neither of them gets our full attention.

⁂ Computers were supposed to save us time. Instead, they simply demand that we do more faster and always. It is time for a revolution.

❋ Fortunately, no one is ever stuck in any one stage of life—cemented in that ignorance, smothered in the arrogance appropriate to an earlier time. Instead, we grow old: life's singular blessing. Or as Sara Teasdale says, "Time is a kind friend; he will make us old."

❋ Time is made for more than doing. It is also made for joy, for fun, for friends, and for finding new ways to enjoy life. Don't forget this year to give those things at least as much attention as you give the others. "Whiskey and music, I reflected," Jean Stafford wrote, "especially when taken together, made time fly incredibly fast."

❋ To be time-bound is to worry every minute of your life: Will the meeting start on time? Will we get out in time? Will we have time to get everything done? Will I be on time for the next appointment? And round and round and round again. There is a calmer, better, more serene way to go through life. Just remember, as Alice Caldwell Rice says, "It ain't no use putting up your umbrella till it rains."

❋ Time is a kind teacher. It enables us to correct every mistake we make. Take advantage of it always. It's so much easier than taking the time to justify every error.

❋ Time is what fools us into thinking that we have forever to be stubborn or unkind or destructive or judgmental of others. But if we don't, then what?

❋ It's not possible to love life and live as if you don't, as if there is no time for living instead of simply existing. "Dost thou love life?" Benjamin Franklin wrote. "Then do not squander time; for that is the stuff life is made of."

❋ Life is an exercise in the spiritual, the beautiful, the relational, and the physical. Which one are you? Which one are you most likely to ignore? This can be

the year to change that, to really begin to
live all of life instead of only part of it.

✳ When we live more in the past than the present, we lag behind our own development.

✳ When we live more in the future than in the
present, we spend life on what doesn't exist
and, more importantly, may never exist.

✳ When we ignore the present, we barter all
the life we may ever have again. "The first
thing necessary for a constructive dealing with time," the psychiatrist Rollo May
writes, "is to learn to live in the reality of the
present moment. For, psychologically speaking, this present moment is all we have."

✳ The great temptation of life is to spend our
time saving up what we'll leave behind. But
what we leave behind will never make up
for what we missed while we were here.

❄ Time is the thief that leads us to cavalierly dismiss the present in favor of a future that never comes.

❄ Time is meant to give us the opportunity for life, not the mistake of ignoring it. "Time wasted," Edward Young writes, "is existence; time used is life."

❄ It is a mistake to try to stop time, to resist change, to stop the kinds of development needed in each age and stage of life. It is also spiritual immaturity.

❄ When you're tempted this year to make time your God, remember that wag who, when asked to define time, said with more wisdom than intelligence something it could behoove us all to remember: "Time," he wrote on the sidewalk, "is what keeps everything from happening all at one time." Hmmph.

Chapter Six

Progress

Time has two aspects. There is the arrow,
the running river, without which there
is no change, no progress, or direction,
or creation. And there is the circle or
the cycle, without which there is chaos,
meaningless succession of instants, a world
without clocks or seasons or promises.
Ursula K. Le Guin

Trust me: there have been few weeks like this one. The weather on the Dead Sea was damp and muggy; the conference hall, beautiful in the most Arabic of solid, gilded ways, was nevertheless a warren of endless marble halls and high ceilings and lush gardens and outlying residence halls. More, the conference presentations were in one of three languages. The situation, in other words, was difficult enough to negotiate without adding the impossible to it. But in the Middle East the impossible is the order of the day.

In the midst of a conference on peace, justice, and reconciliation, another Israeli raid on a terrorist house in Gaza left fifteen dead and 300 of the poorest of the poor homeless.

For a moment, all the progress achieved in trying to bring together women from opposite cultures to work for peace seemed to have been for nothing. Forget the positive group reports; never mind the glimmers of mutual respect; pay no attention to all the promises of email contacts and ongoing relationships. There was only one question in everybody's mind now: would this latest violence only make the Israeli women more anxious, and the Palestinian women more angry? Would we be back in the vortex of "You stop the terrorism and we'll stop the wall"—"You stop the wall and we'll stop the terrorism"?

I held my breath.

But suddenly something happened that made me understand the differences Le Guin makes about kinds of time. The arrow—the direct event designed to effect immediate change—had been stopped for a moment, it seemed, suspended in mid-air. The progress toward peace threatened to disappear on the spot. The change we had hoped for in bringing these Israeli and Palestinian women together across borders, across cultures, across agendas, beyond the guns, seemed to have faded like water under the desert sun.

But then without warning, minutes after the announcement and the prayer for the victims, 250 women—Jewish rabbis in their kippas, Palestinians in their veils, Buddhists and Hindus and Christians and politicians and international supporters— stood up, wove a net of hands that bound the whole auditorium into one screen of peace; and in broken English, bad Arabic, halting Hebrew, and a collage of international accents, we sang what I hadn't heard for years: "We Shall Overcome."

The arrow had fallen, yes, but the circle, the reflection, the soulful review of the event, took over and discovered new meaning, another kind of significance in the situation.

Yes, there had been an event that completely

contradicted the very purpose for which we'd come to this place—the making of relationships that could bridge the gap between peoples that this very kind of violence had created.

Yes, it could have unleashed the blaming, the anger, the point and counterpoints of aggression that had kept the anger going all these years.

But, instead of ending with the arrow, the women simply gave way to the other kind of time. They circled back and thought about it for a moment. Then, another kind of meaning emerged: The new violence only proved that we needed peace more than ever, that arrows—actions—weren't enough. It took a recircling of ideas and reflection on events to realize that it is the recommitment of groups and the reinvention of relationships that matter more than ever when actions that look decisive fail to achieve the instant changes for which we dream.

On the spot the group decided that next year the conference will be held in the center of the storm, in Gaza, for all to see that peace is really possible.

❉ The modern world takes the position that change for the sake of change is progress. Where is the proof of that? In nuclear weaponry? In bigger schools? In remote bureaucracies? In the global transmission of smut? In ghettoes and child labor and slavery?

❉ Change without reflection is change without soul.

❉ Time itself is a strange concept. It assumes that the past is old and that the present is new. It fails, far too often, to understand that the present is what it is precisely because of what we did in the past. The only real question is, then, what are we doing now to make the future better?

❉ It is easy to assume that all the actions of the present will be corrected in the future. It is also foolish. Only now determines tomorrow. Violence cannot bring peace; hatred cannot bring reconciliation; aggression cannot bring trust; self-centeredness

cannot bring love and family and personal
success. Until we believe present actions
are the future, nothing will really change.

※ It's the cyclical celebration of feast days
and birthdays and anniversaries that alerts
us to the real meaning of those events. To
take the position that those things are a
waste of time, don't really count, aren't
important, squeezes the juice out of life.

※ Beware the person who tells you simply
to "forget about it." As in, forget about
the hurt, forget about the death, forget
about the loss. There is no such thing as
healthy forgetting till we realize what the
event means in us now. Only then are we
ready for the fine art of getting on in life.

※ Failing to act when action is necessary is to fail to live life to the fullest.
Failing to take counsel about the re-
sults of an action before we take it is to
doom our lives to total superficiality.

❋ The question for a culture that now measures itself in nanoseconds rather than years is: what things can't be rushed by rushing them? Or as James Thurber put it: "Humans are flying too fast for a world that is round. Soon we will catch up with ourselves in a great rear-end collision and we will never know that what hit us from behind was ourselves."

❋ Change and progress are two different things. Change makes today different than yesterday. Progress makes today better than yesterday.

❋ When what I'm doing is right for me — meaning happy for me, fulfilling for me, enriching for me, developmental of me — why would I change it? For more money? For more power? For more prestige? Be careful. As Edward Abbey points out, "Growth for the sake of growth is the ideology of the cancer cell."

⁂ When we try to pin events down to our liking, to keep things just as they have always been, we run the risk of refusing to see what can be. "I have great belief in the fact that whenever there is chaos," Septima Clark writes, "it creates wonderful thinking. I consider chaos a gift."

⁂ Le Guin is right. There must be periods of action in life but there must also be periods of reflection on what they really mean, on what has happened to us as a result of them. Each needs the other. Each of them, alone, is incomplete.

⁂ Fear is the great impediment to life. "I dreamed a thousand new paths," the Chinese say. "I woke and walked my old one." The question is: why?

⁂ Woe to us when we lose the capacity for restlessness and discontentment. It is a sign that we have lost the taste for life. We have given in to stagnancy. "Restlessness

and discontent," Thomas Edison said,
"are the necessities of progress."

❊ Trying to hold life down, being content to
go on when going on in the same way has
long been fruitless, only robotizes the soul
and makes us more machines than humans.

❊ The sign of real progress is enrichment.
When I and my world are deeper, kinder,
softer, stronger as a result of change, that is
progress. When all change does is to feed the
parts of me that are hard or selfish or short-
tempered or crass, it is time to give new
thought to what we're doing. "Those who
speak most of progress," Santayana wrote,
"measure it by quantity and not by quality."

❊ If my life isn't better and more meaningful
now than it was four years ago, despite all the
change, all the events, all the filling of time
with things, then the circle of time, the pursuit of meaning, needs to be cultivated again.

❋ An event is only bad if we fail to become better because of it.

❋ There is no such thing as unending progress. There is only the kind of progress that leads us to stop doing what we're doing so we can do something better.

❋ Every event has its extreme, its end, the point at which to do more of it is worse, not better. To fail to contemplate those end points in life is to watch the soul go to dust. When is money too much money? When is my desire for security actually the cause of my insecurity? When is my love for the other destructive of myself? When is achievement loss? Without respect for, a commitment to, cyclic time, I'll never know. And then it will be too late.

❋ Daring to do things differently in life is what gives life the lilt of music, the spice of curry, the odor of jasmine, and the edge of the blade.

❋ We must learn to obey whatever it is in us that desires to be different so that what we have too long taken for granted—war, oppression, poverty, enmity—might surrender to the best in all of us.

❋ The most important quality of life is to bring the two aspects of time—the running river and the circle—into harmony. Then what we're doing will have a far greater quality than either "progress" or "success." It will have meaning.

❋ My attitude toward time determines my contributions to life. I can be a doer of events, no matter how useless. Or I can be a thinker of thoughts, no matter how inane. Or I can be a doer who measures all my actions on the basis of their eternal value. Then I become the kind of person who refuses to strike the first blow. Then I'm a bringer of peace.

Chapter Seven

Dignity

How refreshing, the whinny of a packhorse
unloaded of everything! *Zen saying*

P eople bring clothes to the community's
soup kitchen regularly. Some of it goes to
specific families in need. Most of it goes
to our soup kitchen guests themselves. There are
winter coats, children's jackets, assortments of
shoes and slacks and shirts and hats. All of it comes
in clean and pressed, some of it new and unused,
the labels still on the sleeves.

If you watch carefully you will see it go down
the block later: lime green jackets over maroon
pants, ball caps over suit coats, long women's coats
over bulky jeans. The women wearing it are push-

ing shopping carts that hold everything else they own. The men carry their life possessions in green garbage bags over their shoulders, or they simply wear one set of clothes till it wears out before they try on another set.

That kind of "clothing the naked" is relatively easy. What is not easy is clothing the people who must wear it with the kind of dignity such clothes are meant to display.

There is, at the same time, a kind of poverty even more difficult to deal with than the need for clothes by those whose lives lack the means it takes to pick and choose, to save or give away, to mix and match their way through life. In fact, it is the dignity—the humanity—that those stripped naked of soul and psyche, body and reputation, most stand to lose in a world that lacks compassion. It is that kind of exposure which, in the end, strips us all down to the core of who we really are. We sell newspapers on this kind of nakedness daily. The headlines read:

Socialite family shattered
by expensive divorce case

Mentally ill man jailed for public exposure

Teenager abandoned by parents
too poor to buy food

Woman executive found living in family car

Rape details released to press

Suspect's background reviewed
on evening news

It never ends, this exploitation of emotions, this public disclosure of private information, this parading of embarrassing data that serves no possible purpose. It is, at best, simply the lurid description of irrelevant information that has nothing whatsoever to do with the common good or general welfare or civic government or social issues but can, nevertheless, mark people for life. No, this is information useful only to incite the voyeurs and degenerates. It leads people to hide themselves when they can't hide the facts.

It is the stripping naked of the vulnerable, the public lashing of the innocent, the diminishment of the underprivileged, that is the eternal marking of a soul and a life in progress.

On each chest the world paints a huge A for alcoholic, a great P for petty pilferer, a large S for sexual sinner, a bright V for victim, a black V for vulnerable. And every time we do it, we expose ourselves—our smallness of soul and ideals, our destructiveness of the other, our own lack of security that leads us to build ourselves up by tearing other people down. And then we make ourselves smaller than the little people whose little pitfalls have been made too large to overcome in life.

....

❋ To give dignity to those society deprives of it covers our nakedness as well as theirs.

❋ When we deal tenderly with the lack in others, we make room for a new kind of greatness in ourselves.

❋ Those who take delight in the ridicule of others are those who fear the unmasking of their own inadequacies.

✳ There is nothing holy in pointing out the weaknesses of others. There is, in fact, only the admission of the jealousy that eats away at our own innards. Colossians is clear about the relationship between goodness in ourselves and our goodness toward others: *Because you are God's chosen ones, holy and beloved, clothe yourselves with heartfelt mercy, with kindness, humility, gentleness and patience* (Colossians 3:12).

✳ Those who thrive on the insufficiencies of others only prepare their own downfall, the moment at which the world sees through them. Inspired by their own sense of self-righteousness, they put their own weaknesses on display. "All are naked, none is safe," Marianne Moore writes. It is a lesson worth remembering, for our own sakes.

✳ Those who have nothing have only us to supply for them. They wait for a healing hand to lift them up. "Do you want to honor Christ's body?" John Chrysostom writes. "Then do

62

not despise him when you see him naked,
and do not honor him here in church by
wearing silk, while you neglect him outside
the church where he is cold and naked."

❋ The poor are among us so that we cannot
be condemned by our unmerited wealth.

❋ There is no nakedness that can possibly obscure the essential worth of any
and every human being. "Human nature has ineffable dignity," John Duns
Scotus wrote. There is no person below
us, and none is above us either. We will
be judged both on our respect for others
and on our sense of the equality of all.

❋ When we deride another person, mock
them, make fun of them, strip them of
their essential dignity, we expose the por-
nographic emptiness of our own souls.

❋ When we have nothing that masks us, that
makes us look like what we are not, then

we have everything. Then there is nothing anyone can take from us that will leave us bereft or embarrassed or undone.

✳ Don't worry about what anyone will say about your past. Worry only about the authenticity of your present self-presentation.

✳ To misrepresent your age or your economic status or your professional credentials or your social situation is to have failed to come to grips with yourself. We can only be the best of what we are. Nothing less. Nothing more.

✳ Being willing to take everyone we meet at face value, to resist evaluating them against false norms, to treat them as equals, to honor their gifts, is a sign of our own security, our own genuineness, our own quality of soul.

✳ To refuse to respond to the nakedness of another exposes my own. "Decorate yourself from the inside out," Andrei

Turnhollow writes. It is a concept to-
tally foreign to modern society but ab-
solutely imperative to its salvation.

❈ We can only do so much to make ourselves
look better than we are, either physically
or spiritually. Then there is nothing left
but the soul we bring to a situation with its
kindness, its quality, and its openness. Or,
as Glenda Jackson puts it, "I used to believe
that anything was better than nothing. Now
I know that sometimes nothing is better."

❈ True is always better than false—even
where I myself am concerned. "If most
of us are ashamed of shabby clothes and
shoddy furniture," Einstein wrote, "let
us be more ashamed of shabby ideas
and shoddy philosophies...It would be
a sad situation if the wrapper were better than the meat wrapped inside it."

❈ The props of life—titles, uniforms, rank,
cars, clothes, houses, social circles—are only

that: the little marks we use to let people know how important we are. It's what we are without them that really matters.

✳ Those who are stripped of the props of life—money, things, reputation, education, professional rank—stand naked in our midst to show us what we ourselves would be without them.

✳ What we wear makes us forget what we are—or pretend to be more than we are. "What a strange power there is in clothing," Isaac Bashevis Singer writes, "which ought to lead us to wonder how many geniuses are sitting on park benches unemployed, unnoticed, and untapped for their social resources while society ignores them to its peril."

✳ When we fail to clothe children with education and the arts, culture will eventually leave all of us naked of dignity and stripped of social impact.

⁂ It isn't so much that we are naked that matters. What matters more is what we choose
to cover ourselves with as we go through life.

⁂ When we make no room in our
lives for those who are least like us,
we are most naked of reality.

⁂ Jesus is the great model of what it is to be
genuine. In a stable, in a manger, in the
cold, without retinue, without fanfare,
without signs and symbols of public sta-
tion and public import, Jesus came. And
the world around him changed forever.

⁂ Burying ourselves in things only serves to
hide us—even from ourselves. As the philosopher Simone Weil said: "Attachment
is a manufacturer of illusions and whoever
wants reality ought to be detached."

⁂ Better to walk through life simply and
without masks, than to lose ourselves
in the pursuit of identities that are

purely cosmetic and commercial. Then,
at least, we will be known for what we
are rather than for what we are not.

❊ What we fail to seek and to value in others is what is missing in our own souls. If
we discount honesty and beauty, effort and
sincerity, simplicity and kindness in those
around us, it is we who are naked of these
things. It is we who miss the meaning of life.
"Our dignity," George Santayana writes, "is
not in what we do, but what we understand."

❊ In clothing the nakedness of others,
we array ourselves in qualities too profound to mention but too powerful to
be missed by the rest of the world.

Chapter Eight

Hope

SINCE THE HOUSE IS ON FIRE,
LET US WARM OURSELVES.
Italian proverb

It isn't the way I would have wanted to learn the lesson, I admit, but at the same time, I know when I look back that it is certainly one of the more valuable insights I ever discovered in life.

The year that would later be described as the last of the great polio epidemic in the United States was at its height. Polio hospitals everywhere were full. Every day they brought new patients in on gurneys — grown men, small children, infants, women of all ages. I was one of that year's statistics myself.

There were no rooms left in the infectious disease hospital to which they were now taking polio patients, and the wards were full as well.

The thirteen other women in the ward were all older, one just newly married, most of them mothers of young children.

Most of the children had already been transported to the Shriners children's hospital in the area.

Down the hall, the men's ward was full too.

Just sixteen, too young for adult rehabilitation and too old for the children's units, I felt lost, scared, angry, and very, very alone. Depression hung like morning mist over the place. It was in the air you breathed, the smell that clung to the walls. No one walked with a light step here. In fact, no one walked here at all.

Instead, we were all there, strangers quarantined together, voices low, talk limited.

I could hear the woman in the corner sniffling. She cried all day every day, and all night too. The others lay on their sides in silence. One woman struggled to control a pair of knitting needles—the task, I learned later, that had been her physical therapy for months. Then one day, one of the men came rolling into the room, tilting the wheels on his chair in a rakish, boyish way.

"Anybody wanna race?" he called down the center aisle of the ward. "We're getting ready."

"Just get out of here!" the woman said between sniffles. And then she sobbed, "I just want privacy! Even my husband wouldn't barge in on me like this."

The man in the wheelchair looked at her for a moment and shook his head.

"I do," I said. "I want to race. But I don't have a wheelchair."

"Don't worry, kid. We'll be back as soon as you get one," he said as he spun his chair around and rolled back out the door.

Those wheelchair races saved me. I never won any of them but my arms got stronger by the week and I learned to handle the chair. And, most of all, I laughed a lot and made new friends and had a great sense of the possible that carried me for years. I learned that the Italians are right. It isn't what happens to us that counts. It's what we do with what happens to us that makes all the difference.

❋ No one but ourselves can decide for us what every day of our life will be like. As Hubert Humphrey said, "Oh, my friend, it's not what they take away from you that counts. It's what you do with what you have left."

❋ "Sometimes you gotta *manufacture* enthusiasm," the football announcer insisted. "You gotta put a little pep in your step, a little pride in your stride," he lamented as the team of the week slipped further and further behind. People pay big money to hear that from motivational speakers. The only difference is that football teams get paid to do it. The rest of us just get to go on living—whichever way we choose.

❋ Going on when going on seems useless is of the essence of character—and the ground of personality.

❋ It's not losing something—like money, for example—that destroys a person. It depends on what you think about money to begin with that determines the quality of your life.

❊ "You possess only what cannot be lost in
a shipwreck," the Sufi say. And yet we live
as if it were everything else that counted.

❊ Viktor Frankl, speaking of those in the
concentration camps who devoted their
lives to keeping up the spirits of those
around them, wrote: "Everything can be
taken from us but one thing: the last of the
human freedoms—to choose one's attitude in any given set of circumstances."

❊ The central exercise of life is to refuse
to be depressed at least once a day, however depressing the circumstance in which
we find ourselves at that moment.

❊ When all I do is fume about what isn't, I
lose a lot of life in which I could be rejoicing
instead about all the good things that are.

❊ It's one thing to hope that things will go

our way. It's another thing entirely to demand that they do. The person who hopes,
adjusts. The person who demands, pouts.

❊ Nothing lasts forever, we know. So
there is nothing irrational about hop-
ing for better times always.

❊ It's not that initial responses to a situation—like anger, for instance—are unacceptable. It's just that, for the sake of our
own mental health if nothing else, we
can't afford to stay that way forever.

❊ It's not necessary to win all of life's contests,
but it is necessary to go on doing the best
we can. "Life only demands from you the
strength you possess," Dag Hammarskjold
wrote. "Only one feat is possible—not to
have run away." That in itself—to refuse
to give in to the natural discouragement
of the moment—is reason to rejoice.

❊ Being able to distinguish between want

and need may be one of the most important of life's lessons. It is the difference between satisfaction and unbridled ambition. "Riches are not from the abundance of worldly goods," the Prophet Mohammed said, "but from a contented mind."

✳ We are the source of our own suffering, the Buddha teaches. When we fail to curb our desires, when we refuse to live life with a relaxed grasp, we doom ourselves to the demon discontent.

✳ "See the birds of the air," Jesus said. "They neither reap nor sow yet our God gives them what they need." Faith is knowing that what I'm going through right now is providing something my soul needs and without which I will never grow to full stature as a human being. And that changes our attitude toward everything.

✳ The goal is not to go through life like some kind of smiling, unfeeling robot. If a situation is sad, wrong, disgusting, destructive, of course we should realize that. But we must not allow ourselves to be destroyed by it.

❈ The emotional goal of a healthy life is to learn to realize that though our first response to anything may definitely be correct, we don't have to get stuck there. We are not powerless to think differently, to think otherwise, to think of something else.

❈ The most dangerous thing in life is the possibility of allowing ourselves to get stuck in our own negative emotions.

❈ Once we have gone through the worst thing in life we can imagine—and survived it—we are free forever. After that, nothing we fear can ever trap us in despair again. As Albert Camus put it: "In the midst of winter, I finally learned that there was in me an invincible summer."

❈ Life changes from good to bad, from

bad to good all the time. The important thing is to have a center that is impassive to both. "Birds sing after a storm," Rose Kennedy, after years of tragedy, wrote. "Why shouldn't people feel as free to delight in whatever remains to them?"

※ One of the most important things to remember is that each of us has the ability to pollute the atmosphere in which we live. The question is only whether I make the environment around me better for other people—or worse.

※ We each get to decide whether or not we will collapse in the face of difficulty, curl up in a ball and lick our wounds forever, or get up and go on—in a different direction, perhaps, but on. Always on.

※ Life is a mixture of what we like and what we don't. The thing to remember is that both of them form us and that without either we are likely to become very different people.

❊ It is not only how we ourselves react that is important. It's the feelings we feed in others that mark us as worthy friends and fully adult companions. "Just as despair," Elie Wiesel writes, "can come only from other human beings, hope, too, can be given to one only by other human beings."

❊ Everybody needs to dream the dream of a better life, a better world. But there is such a thing as failing to accept life as it is to the point that we miss what's good about it too. "The greatest part of our happiness," Martha Washington wrote, "depends on our dispositions, not our circumstances."

❊ Life is about learning to quit complaining about everything. Or as Jack Benny said, "I don't deserve this award, but I have arthritis and I don't deserve that either." When we come to realize that life is a series of events—good, bad, and indifferent—we will learn to deal with all of them better.

Chapter Nine

Feasting

ONE OF THE VERY NICEST THINGS ABOUT LIFE
IS THE WAY WE MUST REGULARLY STOP
WHATEVER IT IS WE ARE DOING
AND DEVOTE OUR ATTENTION TO EATING.
Luciano Pavarotti

O ne day in one of those great life inventory games that have become so popular in an age of humanistic psychology and personal development exercises, I was part of a seminar that asked us to list ten of your warmest memories. It was easy. I wrote them all down quickly:

1. Family birthday parties
2. My mother's Irish potato candy at Christmastime
3. Summer picnics on the peninsula

4. Thanksgiving dinner
5. Dad's cinnamon toast
6. Packing sandwiches for our fishing trips together
7. Watermelon on the Fourth of July
8. Our family's Irish wakes and the storytelling times we had there
9. Eating out on the weekends
10. Smelling my mother's oyster stew

It didn't take long before I realized that it wasn't the food that I remembered. It was the occasion and all it meant, year after year after year. All those things had marked my way through life. They were the things I waited for. They were the moments that made life special, and family real and life fun. The food was simply the sign that all those things were still safe, still functioning, still the stuff of life.

Then, years later, I began to understand that even the liturgical calendar was a virtual excursion into the way to live life. We learned early in the novitiate the distinction between first- and second-class feasts and feria days. In the early Middle

Ages, in a period when there were no such things as public holidays, no way to relieve the burden of the poor, the Church had begun to insert moments in life that required people to live differently than the social burdens of the time demanded.

The Church made life fun, and feasting a holy act.

First-class feasts—the great feast days of the church: Christmas, Easter, Pentecost, the Assumption, the Ascension—were a time when work stopped for everyone—for the slaves, for the peasants, for the poor, as well as for the rich.

In the community, we called them "speaking days."

They were (except for Easter and Pentecost, of course) weekdays with the character of Sundays. Everything in life relaxed a bit. Liturgy was more beautiful, more ornate, more artistic, more joyful. The community spoke both during the day and at meals. There was always something special on the table: pie, homemade cinnamon rolls, raisins in the morning oatmeal.

Second-class feasts were the feasts of the great saints. On these days there were special feast-day parties or pilgrimages or blessings or gatherings.

Local patron saints — St. Walburga and St. Paul, St. Joseph and St. Cecilia, St. Michael and St. Christopher — were honored in a special way in the liturgy, and people celebrated their lives with great festivals and public events. Vestiges of those feasts still exist in cultures around the world.

The rest of the liturgical calendar, feria days, were life as usual. Food was simple; work was steady and, for the most part, physical. The liturgical feast days provided the only rest most people ever got. And the western world lived from feast to feast because of them.

We don't live like that anymore. We have forty-hour weeks and long weekends and civic holidays, as well as liturgical feast days by which to pace our lives, to redirect our minds, to remember what life is really about when all the work is finished.

We have learned that feasting, as well as fasting, is a necessary dimension of life.

The oyster stew and the watermelon, the fresh bread for sandwiches, and the bottle of wine to go with them, the smell of a Christmas ham and a turkey on Thanksgiving, the weekly meal with the crowd, the holidays and birthdays and picnics and family specialties—all serve to remind us still of the glory of God, the bounty of God, the blessedness of life, the proof that life, in the end, is always good.

....

❉ There are times when it seems that life will never be good again, that this pain will never go away. That is exactly the moment when we most need to remember the good moments, the great laughter, the sweet tastes of yesterday that always, always come again.

❉ Learning to celebrate life is one of the best lessons a person can learn. We need to teach children to celebrate the great moments of life so that they see their responsibility to maintain them.

❉ We are not spoiling children by giving them treats. We are simply immersing them in the joy of life so that they are never tempted to despair of it.

❉ Workaholics stand perched on the edge

of forgetting that most of the good things
of life come to those others who are willing to sit and watch the grass grow while
they enjoy what grew without their effort.

☀ It's important to dot our lives with un-
scheduled as well as scheduled feast days.
That way we remember that we are able
to make joy as well as to expect it. Or as
Lin Yutang, the Chinese philosopher,
put it: "Our lives are not in the lap of
the gods, but in the lap of our cooks."

☀ Celebrations are an excuse to enjoy the
world and to enable others to enjoy it too.

☀ If you want to know whether or not you're
living a balanced life, ask yourself whether
your feasting and your fasting—your sense of
praise and trust—come in common measure.

☀ Food and feasting are the things that remind us of the unending glory, the limitless love, of God. Voltaire said of it:

"Nothing would be more tiresome than eating and drinking if God had not made them a pleasure as well as a necessity."

❋ A Jewish proverb teaches us that "worries go down better with soup." Treating food as a sacrament rather than a necessity reminds us that, in the end, there is always more good in life than bad. The trick is to notice it.

❋ To love good food is a measure of our love of life. Food preparation teaches us to do everything we can to make life palatable, spicy, comforting, full of love.

❋ Cooking for other people is the way we wish them well for tomorrow and enable them to attain it.

❋ Sitting down to a meal with the family— table set, food hot, salad fresh, water cold, dishes matched, and food served rather than speared—may be the very foundation of family life in which we celebrate our need for one another. The loss of the family feast may do more to loosen the family bonds than any other single dimension of family life.

❋ What cupboard doesn't have a collection of recipes carefully gathered down through the ages, adjusted over the years, scavenged from the underside of every conversation? Such are the things that bind us to one another. "I refuse to believe that trading recipes is silly," Barbara Grizzuti Harrison says. "Tuna fish casserole is at least as real as corporate stock."

❋ How is it possible to have a feast if we don't know the difference between the taste of a fresh tomato and a hothouse tomato, a homemade pickle and a factory pickle, fresh bread from packaged bread?

❋ One purpose of feasting is to get back in touch with the earth that sustains us, to glorify the God that made it, and to pledge ourselves to save the land that grows our food.

※ Feasting is what connects us not only to the people with whom we celebrate this moment but with the rest of the world as well. It is an act of human community. "Cutting stalks at noontime," the Chinese poet Chan-Pao writes, "perspiration drips to the earth. Know you that your bowl of rice each grain from hardship comes?"

※ Every meal well done, well served, well spiced, well savored, well spent, is a feast. There is no need for a great deal of money, just a great deal of care.

※ In this country, we are conditioned to think that taking time to eat together, to make a meal an event rather than an act, takes time from the important things of life. That may be exactly why we are confused now about what the important things of life really are. "Happiness," Astrid Alauda writes, "is a bowl of cherries and a book of poetry under a shade tree."

❊ I have a friend who follows the sun around her back yard in a deck chair with a glass of fresh fruit juice in one hand and a book in the other. Here's the question: Is she "wasting" time or "celebrating" time? Think carefully before you answer. It can get to be a very important question as life goes by.

❊ Good food is the hallmark of every season: fresh fruit in summer, roasted chestnuts in the fall, warm bread in winter, oyster stew in the spring. Leslie Newman says of it: "As the days grow short, some faces grow long. But not mine. Every autumn, when the wind turns cold and darkness comes early, I am suddenly happy. It's time to start making soup again." Good food is the sacrament of life everlasting.

❊ Food doesn't have to be exotic to be wonderful. Peasant societies give us some of the best meals ever made. It is always simple, always the same—and always different due to the subtle changes of sauce and cook-

88

ing style that accompany it. As the Polish say: "Fish, to taste right, must swim three times—in water, in butter, and in wine."

- To be feasted is to be loved outrageously.

- A fast-food life is a life that misses life entirely.

- Feasting is a divine imperative. It says, "Thou shalt not ignore the joys of life."

- Fasting is an important discipline because it teaches us to say "no" to our impulses. Feasting is an important discipline because it teaches us to say "yes" to life.

- The farmer's market is a tribute to life grown here, lived here, to be celebrated here. It links us with ourselves.

Chapter Ten

Happy endings

JIDDU KRISHNAMURTI, ONE OF THE MOST
REVERED SPIRITUAL TEACHERS OF THIS CENTURY,
ONCE ASKED A SMALL GROUP OF LISTENERS
WHAT THEY WOULD SAY TO A CLOSE FRIEND
WHO IS ABOUT TO DIE. THEIR ANSWERS DEALT
WITH ASSURANCES, WORDS ABOUT BEGINNINGS
AND ENDINGS, AND VARIOUS GESTURES OF
COMPASSION. KRISHNAMURTI STOPPED THEM
SHORT. "THERE IS ONLY ONE THING YOU CAN SAY
TO GIVE THE DEEPEST COMFORT," HE SAID. "TELL
HIM THAT IN HIS DEATH A PART OF YOU DIES AND
GOES WITH HIM. WHEREVER HE GOES, YOU GO
ALSO; HE WILL NOT BE ALONE."

As told by Larry Dossey

The sunflowers seemed to go to seed early this year. Thomas—potter to the world, brother to us—died in the quiet way he'd always lived and will be buried soon in the urn he made for himself after the surgery proved futile. And in the midst of it, another friend struggles with a diagnosis that defies itself at every turn. No doubt about it. The signs are clear everywhere: The shadows of life are longer now. Even the grass has seared a bit. And with the changing of the climate and the dulling of the sun and the lengthening of the nights, something inside ourselves slows and changes and turns as well. With the turning of the seasons of our lives, life takes on a far more precious hue.

It is the season of memories now. It is the time of year that piques hope and prods it to doubt. It is, then, the time of the year in which resurrection takes on a new kind of meaning. Yes, things die and, no, nothing ever dies because, yes, it goes on living again in us.

Death seems so cruel, so purposeless, at times. But it's not. Death is what alerts the rest of us to life—just when we have grown tired of it ourselves, perhaps, or worse yet, simply unaware of it at all.

Death is the call to look again at life—this time with a wiser eye. Life, for the likes of us, is not a series of struggles and irritations. That, it seems, is reserved for refugees and farm families on hard soil and peasant types on mountaintops and peons in barrios. Our life, on the other hand, is a panoply of opportunities. It does not depend on "luck." It depends on what we do with it, how we approach it, what we make of what we have, how we distinguish between wants and needs—and, most of all, how much of ourselves we put into making it better, not only for ourselves, but for those who lack the resources even to begin to make it better for themselves.

Death, the awareness of its coming, the sounds of it around us, is what calls us to a life beyond apathy, beyond indifference, beyond unconcern. Death reminds us to live.

This is the period when the parts of us that died with the death of those we loved rise again in the recollection of past moments and the tears of past tendernesses. This is when we know for certain that every deed we ever do lives on somewhere in someone who remembers it. This is when we are made to see death as a prod to life.

The death of the year, the death of the past, begins to bloom again in old memories and the lessons we learned from them, in long-known truths and newly realized loves, in new perceptions of past obscurities.

The time is short for all those things. The time is now. The time is for reflection on what we've lost in life, yes, but for what we have left in life too. It's time to begin to live life fuller rather than faster.

Death gives us all the gift of time — our own and the time of those around us. It calls us to stop and look at sunflowers next time, to care for the grass always, to embrace the planet forever, to pay attention to our friends, to take comfort in the dark, to remember that the daffodils will unfold again. It is time to plant spring in our own hearts, to remember "the light that no darkness can take away."

Then, when death comes for us, as it surely will, we will know that it is only prelude. "I don't know what's there," the dying old woman said to her grieving friend. "I only know that God is there. So, don't worry. That is enough."

✳ Death does not dampen life. It simply reminds us to live the rest of it well. "Some people," Henry Van Dyke wrote, "are so afraid to die that they never begin to live."

✳ Life we get for free. Who we are when we die, we must earn.

✳ Death is not only an enemy. It is a friend as well who releases us from pain, from diminishment, from solitude. We must learn to celebrate that too.

✳ We must learn to remember when we are at our most passionate, our most stubbornly closed to the other, that we are both dying: they and we. Is this the way we want to do it?

✳ Life is too short to spend whining, weeping, stamping our feet. "There are those," the Buddha says in the Dhammapada, "who forget that death will come to all. For those who remember, quarrels come to an end."

❋ We waste too much of life worrying about death. It is as natural as birth and twice as exciting, twice as mysterious.

❋ Death offends our sense of freedom and self-will. But, then, we have no idea of how liberating this birth into new life may possibly be.

❋ Pity is not the real response to death: It is wonderment; it is fear; it is surrender.

❋ When someone we love dies, we do not weep for them. We weep for ourselves. But oh, how long it takes to admit it.

❋ The major question at the death of another is not "Where did they go?" but "What did they do while they were here that eases the passage before them?"

❋ Death is its saddest when the life that precedes it is of no great account to anyone. "I am not afraid of death," Isabell Eberhardt writes, "but I would not want to die in some obscure or pointless way."

❋ Death is no more to be feared than life. And life, whatever its struggles, we call precious, we call wonderful, we call gift. And why not the journey to the next one?

❋ We say we believe in an afterlife. But when a person dies, we do not say, "I wonder what they will do now?" Instead, we say, "I hope they did enough to merit the glory to come." Now what do you suppose that means?

❋ Only when we are old enough to realize that death is the end of life are we really able to live life thoughtfully, to make every moment count, to repair our broken past by living the present better than ever.

❋ Death is the final realization that life has been good. The trick to a life well lived is to come to that awareness as soon as possible.

✳ If we spend too much of life worrying about death, we can lose a lot of life. If we spend too little of life thinking about death, we can lose a lot of life as well.

✳ Death is the common denominator of the human race. Whatever we are, we are simply just like everyone else. Mortality is the great leveler of pride and prejudice, of profit and power.

✳ The promise of death makes all the deadly things of life bearable.

✳ Life we learn as we go along—death, too. It is the last great mystery of humankind. It takes us to the very edge of nothingness, excited.

✳ The fear of our own death has the capacity to make us kind. The Buddhist Dhammapada teaches: "All beings tremble before danger, all fear death. When we consider this, we do not kill or cause to kill."

❋   It is the very finality of death that persuades us of its purpose. How could something as beautiful as life ever really die? As Winston Churchill put it: "I remember the story of the old man who said on his deathbed that he had had a lot of trouble in his life, most of which had never happened."

❋   When death comes, understanding comes with it. "Is death the last step?" Walter Scott asked—and then answered clearly, "No, it is the final awakening."

❋   Death is neither to be sought nor resisted. It is only to be accepted as the exclamation point of life. "Do not seek death," Dag Hammarskjold wrote, "but seek the road which makes death a fulfillment."

❋   Because we cannot see what happens after death, we are all the more attentive to what happens before it.

❋ We prepare for death by living well all the little deaths along the way. Then we learn that there is always new life on the other side of our worst fears. "It is not dying," Margot Asquith writes, "but living that is a preparation for death."

❋ Every death calls us to a new spring in life.

❋ Epictetus teaches, "For it is not death or hardship that is a fearful thing, but the fear of death and hardship." It is death that teaches us how useless fear really is. Fear of death saps our energy and does nothing whatsoever to bring us to a real appreciation of the kind of life that is beyond length of days.

❋ Death concentrates both the vision and the soul. Or as James Boswell says it, "Depend upon it, Sir, when a man knows he is to be hanged in a fortnight, it concentrates his mind wonderfully."

Chapter Eleven

Yes to life

I thank You God for this most amazing day:
for the leaping greenly spirits of trees
and a blue true dream of sky;
and for everything
which is natural which is infinite
which is yes.

E.E. Cummings

W here I live, winter is a raw and bitter,
windswept and white, unpredictable
and uncompromising time of year.
We go from dry, cold, grey days to deep, wet, fro-
zen days. The pavement turns from white snow
to black ice from one moment to the other. The
wind howls around the house, whipping wet leaves

and soft snowflakes with it. One black night everything in sight is fogged in dark; the next morning even the inner city is clear and clean and deep, deep white. Then we stay inside, make popcorn, light the fire, curl up in blankets, and play games.

Indeed, winter, for us, is an experience in the struggles of life, in its twists and turns, in its great challenges and small triumphs. We watch where we walk now; we cling to handrails from place to place; we drive slowly, deliberately, cautiously from corner to corner. We go through life more thoughtfully, more quietly, more prudently—with an eye to what might happen as well as for what is happening. We manage it all quite well, of course, but not cavalierly. Every step in life demands attention then.

Finally, in the north, finally, one day, almost without warning, spring comes. You smell it. You taste it in the air. You watch pregnant trees explode with new bloom. Suddenly. And you know. You know that life has changed, that life is new again.

Around the neighborhood, the windows begin to open, one at a time, tentatively at first, one here, then another one there. Then all at once, it seems, the street is open and bold with life.

Children appear in the middle of the road, bouncing balls, laughing loudly. The corner ice cream stand, weeks early, opens and calls the children out of their small, old houses like the Pied Piper of play. And all us older people feel our limbs loosen a bit and our hearts begin to smile.

It is an exercise in "yes," this slip-slide from winter to spring. Yes to today; yes to tomorrow; yes to life again. We all come out of the tomb of winter, new and bright with promise. It is "yes" to life-time now, however old, however jaded we may be. It is the rediscovery of possibility again.

The turn of the seasons in the north is a kaleidoscope of the seasons of life, of the face of God in time, of the very process of what it means to be alive.

In the seasons we see the story of ourselves played out: early on, life without shape; later, life in pursuit of direction; finally, life on the way to its horizon; at the end, life mellowed, going down into the sea of eternity. Through all of them, like warp and woof, lies the essential pattern, the obligation to say "yes."

Yes, yes, yes, life teaches us to say. Yes, yes, yes, we must learn to say back. Otherwise, we will surely die long before we have ever learned to live.

❋ Ignoring the problems of life is not a solution to them. It is not "yes" to the challenge of the day. It is, at best, only a charade, a game of pretend. As G.K. Chesterton said, "It isn't that they can't see the solution. It is that they can't see the problem."

❋ Remember that life is to be lived—all of it—in all of its layers and longings. Only then will we ever know our own strength and depth of soul.

❋ When we learn to see every flower, hear every bird, we will be closer than we have ever been to being fully alive.

❋ Life is not to be rationed, parceled out, allotted in sensible pieces—a bit of fun, a touch of joy, a glance at love, as little as possible of sorrow. It is to be lived to the hilt, experienced, accepted. "The only thing better than singing," Ella Fitzgerald said, "is more singing."

❋ Say "yes" to all of life. Say it loudly.
Say it fully. Say it with faith that winter cannot last forever and that spring
comes in strange and sudden guise.

❋ The frame of mind we take to every part of life will have a great deal
to do with the way it affects us.

❋ "Two men looked out from prison bars,"
the poem reads. "One saw mud and the
other saw stars." Which says to us: How
do you see your life? The answer to that
simple question determines whether
you are a happy person or a dour one.

❋ The thing about our winter is that it snows.
The thing about spring is that it rains. The
thing about summer is that it's sweltering
hot. The thing about autumn is that it's
dark and cold. Isn't it wonderful? All of it.
Every single different thing that makes us
adjust and enjoy and live life differently.

✳ There was a time when we thought that what happened to us determined the quality of our life. Now we know that it's what we think about our experiences. "The greatest discovery of my generation," William James, the great psychologist, wrote, "is that a human being can alter their life by altering their attitudes of mind."

✳ The personality we bring to life each day determines the climate of it for everyone else. "An optimist," Susan Bissonette wrote, "is the human personification of spring."

✳ It takes a bit of courage to face the seasons, to dress for them properly, to find something we like to do in each of them, to get up the energy to go out into them, head up, shoulders back, and smiling. In fact, it's finding something right about every day of our lives that makes each of them either a positive or a negative event. The choice is ours.

✳ The way we face the day is the kind of day it will be for other people around us. "Attitudes are contagious," Dennis and Wendy Mannering wrote. "Are yours worth catching?"

✳ Most of us don't say "yes" to life at all. Instead, we say either "no" or, worse, "I refuse." Then we wonder why other people are so much happier than we are.

✳ Oscar Wilde, the Irish writer, put it this way: "If you don't get everything you want, think of the things you don't get that you don't want." Point: Life is a lot better than it could be. Maybe we ought to be glad we got what we did.

✳ No, life is not predictable but it is livable if we only concentrate on what we have more than on what we want. "Life is a shipwreck," Voltaire wrote, "but we must not forget to sing in the lifeboats."

❋ We live life well only by throwing ourselves into it. As Dag Hammarskjold put it, "We are not permitted to choose the frame of our destiny. But what we put into it is our own."

❋ The truth is that no one has the perfect life—except those who are perfectly committed to make the best of the one they have.

❋ The trick to having a happy life is to remember that it all comes down to what we ourselves make of the life we have. "The sun shines and warms and lights us and we have no curiosity to know why this is so," Ralph Waldo Emerson says. "But we ask the reason of all evil, of pain, and hunger, and mosquitoes, and silly people."

❋ It's not the thing we're facing that counts. It's the way we look at the thing we're facing—the long commute across town, the change of jobs, the loss of the promotion, the schedule—that makes all the difference in what it does to us. "It's so hard when I have to," Annie Gottlier writes, "and so easy when I want to."

❋ How is it that we find ourselves doing the very same thing that other people are doing but they are glad to do it and we're not? Easy. "We are all in the gutter," Oscar Wilde writes, "but some of us are looking at the stars."

❋ One of the major obstacles to saying "yes" to life may be that we mistake the accidentals of life for the essence of life. Or to put it another way: "Enjoy the little things," Robert Brault says, "for one day you may look back and realize they were the big things."

❋ An anonymous philosopher wrote once: "Anywhere is paradise; it's up to you."